ISBN 978-1-333-21015-1
PIBN 10473975

1 MONTH OF
FREE
READING

at

www.ForgottenBooks.com

By purchasing this book you are eligible for one month membership to ForgottenBooks.com, giving you unlimited access to our entire collection of over 1,000,000 titles via our web site and mobile apps.

To claim your free month visit:

www.forgottenbooks.com/free473975

DOLLARS WANT ME

THE NEW ROAD TO OPULENCE

A Soul Culture Lesson

—BY—

HENRY HARRISON BROWN,

Author of "How to Control Fate through Sugges-
tion," "Not Hypnotism, but Suggestion,"
"Man's Greatest Discovery,"
and Editor of NOW.

Thou hoard'st in vain what Love should spend
—*Whittier*

That man is poor who thinks himself poor
—*Emerson*

PRICE 10 CENTS

"NOW" FOLK,
1437 MARKET STREET, SAN FRANCISCO, CAL.
LONDON:
L. N. FOWLER & CO.,
7, Imperial Arcade, Ludgate Circus, E. C.

To All
Who Would Be Free from the
Grind of Labor

TO THE READER.

This essay upon the Dollar appeared in NOW as one of a series of twelve lessons entitled, "Success and how I won it through Affirmation." It attracted much attention and drew out from its readers many letters. This appreciation has decided "NOW" Folk to reprint it in form for a wider circulation.

This well conserves the purpose for which it was written. I wish to awaken my fellows to a sense of their present possessions and help them to a realization of the Principle which controls Life's expression so that, Living being to them "A fine art," they will cease to look for happiness in some far-off heaven, but will enter into the enjoyment of the one they create *here* and *now*.

It is believed that this little monograph is the first utterance of the thought that each individual has the ability to so radiate his mental forces that he can cause the Dollar to *feel* him, *love* him, *seek* him and thus draw, at will, all things needed for his unfoldment from the Universal Supply.

160613

It will help you to rise above the drudgery of enforced labor and enable you to enter upon the manifold expressions of life with the joy and spontaneity of childhood. This is the thought which comes to you with this, my Lesson of Success.

HENRY HARRISON BROWN.
San Francisco, Cal., May 1, 1903.

"This new Law of Henry Harrison Brown's has given me new strength and power such as few could easily realize."—O HASHNU HARA, Editor of *Wings of Truth*, London, Eng.

OPULENCE
THE DOLLAR SIDE

—

I AM SUCCESS

—

You conquer fate by thought. If you think the fatal thought of men and institutions, you need never pull the trigger. The consequences of thinking inevitably follow.—CARLYLE.

Personal ideals, of necessity, must differ, yet, since money represents objective power, its consideration must enter as a factor into every ideal of success. Money represents Supply. It stands in our thought, for food, clothing and shelter; for books, pictures and companionship; for enjoyment, unfoldment and expression.

The Dollar means opportunity for the realization of high ideals.

Material Supply is a necessity of Life. The Dollar is the concrete representative of this necessity.

The individual must be free and, until the necessities of life are assured, he is not free. Thus the Dollar stands for individual liberty.

Personal liberty finds its basis in pecuniary independence. Financial independence and personal liberty bear very largely the relation of cause and effect. We can almost say that in the popular mind the Dollar confers liberty. In Soul Culture, a mental attitude of superiority to the Dollar results in personal liberty. There is no liberty to him who *feels* himself limited by the want of the Dollar.

Debt is one of the most tyrannical of masters. Mackay well says:—

> "The debtor is ever a shame faced dog
> With his creditor's name on his collar."

There can be no liberty to him who *feels* the slavery of debt.

Into your ideal of Success, therefore, there must be firmly builded this ideal of pecuniary independence.

This independence does not lie in freedom from debt, neither does it lie in large bank accounts nor the possession of property. Monetary success and personal liberty do not go hand in hand. Indeed the average man of wealth is the veriest slave, enslaved to the necessities that his monetary possessions involve, and a worse slave to his fears.

SUCCESS LIES IN THE MENTAL ATTITUDE THAT ARISES FROM THAT SENSE OF PERSONAL POWER WHICH MEETS EVERY CONDITION WITHOUT

ANXIETY. ''Sufficient unto the day is the evil thereof,'' is the thought of the successful man while he enjoys present good.

That cannot be called success which results in ill health and unhappiness, unrest or fear. Eliminate these from your ideal and you have, as a necessity concomitant of success, financial ease.

In the old competitive thought, men sought business and wanted the dollar. Under the New Thought, it is: ''Seek first the kingdom of Good and its right living and all things nesessary to my happiness will be added to me.'' The Soul has only to manifest its drawing power. When the conscious mind lets itself be led or drawn, it will be drawn to what it desires. Desire is the magnet. Let it have its way. Trust in your own Love of Truth and Love of Goodness and never question. That you desire it, is enough. That you desire it, is evidence that it already exists for you on the Soul-side. Be passive to the desire and LET it manifest. This attitude is itself Success and leads to this attitude towards things.

Affirm: THINGS BELONG TO ME. I AM ALREADY POSSESSOR. THEY WILL COME TO ME AT NEED. Then LET them come. If they are not, do not waste time trying for them. Having accepted Truth that ALL IS YOURS and that ALL DESIRED CONDITIONS or THINGS WILL MANIFEST, never think more of them.   LET them come. All looking for things to come evidences that you have not claimed them as realities, but have held them as dreams or possibilities. Until you hold them as realities, they cannot come, unless you give up Thought-drawing and go back to the old competitive struggle, then they may be grasped.

Change your attitude toward business. Do not seek it. SEE IT ALREADY YOURS and LET it come.   Attend yourself to details as they come to the surface.   Consider business a Principle that will run, as runs a mountain stream, when you remove your conscious will from it.   All your concern is to be ready to use it as the ranchman uses the water as it comes to his ditch.

Business is a manifestation of the One Power. Use the Power as the telegrapher uses: LET it come and you direct it.   The wisdom for the day comes with the day.   LET it come by faith in Self.   Work each moment as if it *were* here and it IS here.

In regard to money, regard it also as merely the power that keeps business going.   Welcome its coming and rejoice at its going. It never does its work until, like water in the stream, it has passed under the wheel.

YOU alone are the Power. Money has only delegated Power. You direct its expression. Change your attitude toward money. It is not ''the almighty dollar.'' Almighty Power uses the dollar. Say to the dollar, ''I do not need you. You need me. You are of no use until my brain and hand use you. You wish to be used. You come to me that you may be used. I do not need a dollar. Dollars need me.'' Assume this mental attitude and see what a change it makes for you. When you have changed your aura, dollars will be drawn and you need not think of their coming. Only think of using them.

Change your attitude toward the dollars you have. Tell them they are of no use until they are expended. As you see them lying about, say to them:—''Idle dollars, go to work. Go out and circulate about. Each one of you go and pay a million in wages and debts. When I need you, come back again. You are useless and have no value until you go to work. Then LET them go to work, knowing that, *when you send this thought with them,* they or their fellows will come to you to be set at work.

Before you spend a dollar, the question comes, "Is it right?" Whether you have a single dollar, or behind the one you think of spending are a million, makes no difference. If it is right to spend the dollar in the proposed way, had you the million, it is right thus to spend it when it is the lone one. Therefore, when you feel it is right to spend a dollar for any purpose, spend it as royally as if you were a millionaire. From the Inner Life, this message was given to me years ago: "Let a thought of use stand guard over your purse and then spend freely." Amend this by affirming: "A thought of the righteousness of the spending stands guard over my dollars and I send them forth with blessing." These dollars, like every thought of good you send out, will return to bless, for you do business with thoughts only; dollars are but materialized thoughts. Each dollar in any man's hand represents his thought 'n material form. Send out at all times with your dollars the thoughts you wish to return to you, for what you sow in your dollars, you reap in dollars that either do, or do not, come back to you. Put the thought of Success, Happiness and Health into every dollar that passes out and it will return so laden.

CONSCIENTIOUSNESS THE FIRST NEED

"First have something good, then advertise," said Horace Greely. To meet Success, you must have an Ideal that enlists your full sympathy. You cannot be successful unless you feel that you have a right to succeed. *Feel* that you have something that the world needs. You can then feel that Dollars want you; that through them you can give what you have of value to the world. Feel that Dollars wish you to use them for the accomplishment of your purpose to use them justly. With this ideal, you can conscientiously invite Dollars and they will come. They need your heart, brain and hand that they may benefit the world. Dollars are manifestations of the One Infinite Substance as you are, but, unlike you, they are not Self-Conscious. They have no power till you give them power. Make them *feel* this through your thought-vibrations as you *feel* the importance of your work. They will then come to you to be used. They will not come, nor can you in this Thought draw them, to be hoarded. Use, Helpfulness and Happiness must be in your thought of Success. This held firmly, perseveringly, as your **Affirmation, will turn the current of Dollars your** way. Your thought should be: I possess that which the world wants. Dollars want me to use them in scattering that which I have to bless.

These Affirmations I recommend to be personally held:—DOLLARS LOVE ME. DOLLARS WANT ME. I AM READY TO USE DOLLARS AND THEY FREELY COME TO ME TO BE USED. Make no limit as to the amount. Claim abundance. CLAIM ALL YOU CAN USE FOR GOOD, all that is needed to enable you to be useful and happy. ABUNDANT SUPPLY, be your demand.

TIME A FACTOR

In all your Self-Culture, you are to remember that time is a necessary factor in unfoldment. It is not a measure of duration. This mistake of measuring time by the figures on a dial, will never do in this culture. Time is to be measured by growth. Some may grow more while the hands count twenty-four hours than others in ten times that. Take no thought of time. You have all there is. You are Spirit (or Mind, if you prefer the word) and have all eternity.

Seeds require time to germinate, grow, leave,

bud, bloom, blossom and fruit. Each thought, each change in your ideal, is a seed. It will follow nature's line of evolution.

You will require time as you change your attitude! A period will be required to change your vibrations so that the Dollar will *feel you* and learn that it *wants* you. This period will vary according to your power of concentration and your fidelity to your ideal as couched in the Affirmation; *Dollars want me.* The thought-field is first to be cleared of the weeds of the old thought-sowing and the seeds of the new must germinate and become the forest in the garden of Supply.

Pay no attention to the old conditions. Keep at your Affirmation, knowing that it is the reservoir and every irrigating ditch will fill as soon as water can come down from the reservoir to it.

The echo, "I want dollars," must become still before the real sound of *Dollars want me* can vibrate in your aura.

Know, as the merchant knows that he has that which the people want, that you have that which Dollars want. Advertise in your thought, your hand, your life, your purpose to the Dollar. Tell it that it *wants* all these; that without you, it has no power; that, without you, it can do nothing. Tell it that all that it wants, you have; that it will come to you that it may accomplish its mission. Then, like a patient merchant, wait for your customers. Dollars will soon flock, as do customers to a ''bargain'' counter. The ''Want column'' has attracted them. Use here only the same common-sense, perseverance and patience the successful business man uses and Dollars will find their wants supplied in you, and you will find Supply.

SUPPLY.

"He who dares assert the I,
 May calmly wait
 While hurrying fate
 Meets his demands with sure supply."
 —HELEN WILMANS.

There is neither health nor prosperity without harmony. There is no peace, no health, where there is want, be it want of material Supply, wisdom Supply, or love Supply. Love, Truth and Dollars—these are necessary to human well-being.

Mind, body and estate must be cared for; there must be Harmony between all that there may be health, happiness and prosperity. This harmony is found in merely giving Self, the Soul, its way. Harmony is living in obedience to mental law. It is found in right thinking.

Poverty is the main cause of the unrest, the dis-ease (the un-ease) that afflicts mankind. Remove poverty by right thinking and all attendant evils will disappear. This right thinking means that there shall be on the part of the individual a change of attitude toward the Dollar.

The prevalent attitude is *want for* the Dollar, —belief that Dollars are power. This must be outgrown and the attitude must be that ALL POWER IS IN MAN. Dollars are machines with power delegated to them by man. They are useless without man. DOLLARS WANT ME! is to be the thought of the "Coming man." A few so think now and have obtained mastery of Supply.

It is a legitimate demand on part of each individual that he have enough. Opulence is righteousness.

There is enough in the Universal One from which all *things* materialize, for each one to have enough to meet all desires without robbing any. Infinite Supply is all about us and yet there is want. Whose the fault? Not of The One. It is in ourselves. We have not known how to claim, nor have we claimed our own. The law is simple and it is laid down by the greatest political economist as well as the greatest Mental Scientist the world has in its historic records. He was not a theologian, neither did he deal with questions of a future life, as many seem to think; he was a sociologist and a socialist. He dealt with questions of "the life that now is." His name was Jesus. He gave the Law thus: "Seek first

the Kingdom of God and his righteousness,
and all *things* shall be added unto you.''
Analyze the Law thus:—''Kingdom of God?''
Where? ''Within you.'' ''God is Spirit,''
he said. ''The Kingdom of God'' is then in
the Soul. It is the Ego or Soul of man.
Know thyself as Soul; know thyself as Spirit
—this is the Law. Live rightly, is the mean-
ing of ''his righteousness.'' Live in accord
with your sense of right; obey your own con-
science. Then all *things* shall be yours. *Things*
of whatever kind, of all kinds, are manifesta-
tions of the One Substance. Things are the
same as yourself,—manifestations of the One
God. Dollars are things. Dollars are mani-
festations of the One God.

Plain directions, these: Live true to self;
live spiritually; give the first place in your
thought to the eternal, from which things
come and then all things will come to you at
need.

''First?'' Yes! Not things first, but that
mental condition which controls things. Not
Dollars first, but that mental attitude which
attracts Dollars.

That mental condition is Faith in Self as a
manifestation of Omnipotence, Faith in Self
as a manifestation of the All-Good, Faith in

the Universe as Justice, Faith in the Universal One as entirely Good, Faith in the Life you are, to draw its necessary Supply of things demanded for its highest expression. Then *let* things come. This is all, but it is—God. This is the "straight gate." Few there be that enter in, but all may. Few place things "second." Dollars, position, influence, show, —these in common thought, come "first." But these are results of Power. Become first the Power, become one with the Power and these desired things will come. The ordinary process of business, the customary method of thinking, is to be reversed. Think from inward Power, think from Being. You will then be the Master and things will take their right place. Become "one with God" by recognizing Him as King in your Soul. Listen to Him in the edicts of your Soul. Say, as you thus become negative to the Higher in you, "Now, God, do your work your way! and it will be done satisfactorily to me." No one can fail when he assumes this attitude of Love and Trust. It would be an impotent God, and therefore no-God, that did not work when these conditions are made.

Poverty, like consumption, cold or rheumatism, is a mental condition. It can be cured only by the same means, i. e., Affirmation of Power to cure:—*I am part of the One and, in the One, possess all. I possess all!* Affirm this and patiently wait for the manifestation. You have sown the thought-seed, now, like the rancher, wait for the sprouting and the harvest. It can never fail you when, like him, you trust.

Repeat this Affirmation, no matter what the appearances. No matter if hungry, houseless and alone, affirm:—*God is my Supply. My Supply is Infinite. Dollars want me!* Trust implicitly in the inviolable Law of Cause and Effect. You are Cause; Supply is the Effect that must .follow your Affirmation.

In the past, you have sown poverty-seeds, and are now reaping the crop. You do not enjoy this harvest. Sow, amid these results of previous sowing, Plenty-seeds and Plenty will come. Supply is yours when you sow Supply-seeds. Sow, no matter how seemingly black the conditions. The seeds have God-in-them and cannot fail.

I AM SUPPLIED WITH ALL I NEED FROM INFINITE SUBSTANCE! MY SUPPLY IS INFINITE! ALL I DESIRE IS MINE FROM INFINITE ABUNDANCE! GOD IS MY SUPPLY. SUPPLY NEVER FAILS ME! From these Affirmations, choose the one that fits your case or make one from this thought to fit your condition and state of mind. When made, stick to it as gravity sticks to earth. The Law of Supply is as sure as gravity. In this Affirmation, *All is mine! Dollars want me!*   you have repolarized your aura. You have changed your vibrations and you will draw, as the magnet draws the needle, all you can use. Try it! Never let go of your trust that Dollars, or that for which they stand, will come. Thy Kingdom, O Soul, has come and thy will is done, ,for God and Soul are One.

> "All is mine; 'tis but by asking:
> ·   Ere I make my silent plea
> Life unlocks her richest treasures
> For my waiting eyes to see."

SUPPLEMENT.

—

O Hashnu Hara, editor of *Wings of Truth*, London, in the April, 1903, number of that journal has this to say of "The Law of Opulence": —

"The February issue of NOW contained an article on 'Opulence.' I've read a good many articles on opulence, some have impressed me, some fell flat—flat as a pancake—this one didn't. First of all, it placed all my former theories in a wrong light; my idea was to say 'I WANT.' It is quite true that when I did this I generally *got what I wanted* sooner or later, but H. H. B. says that you must not say, *I want,*—in effect, he says you must affirm, '*I don't want dollars; dollars want me.*' A very little consideration will show this is right; but *consideration* wasn't enough for me—I put it to the test. The first five days, my receipts fell almost to zero, but I was determined to hang on. I *felt* it was right, that the drop in my business was due to the readjustment of the vibrations, for long experience has taught me that you cannot turn round from one method of thought to another very suddenly without disturbing the currents and these have to get re-adjusted to the new rate of vibration before you can work them. The sixth day my patience was amply rewarded; for every one order I had been in the habit of receiving, I got twenty and it has kept up ever since.

"*Now* I never weaken my position by affirming that I want anything. I say it wants me, and I know it will come. It is not any use making that statement, of course, if you DOUBT IT. You must back up your statement with faith and feel it is already yours. It is rather on the principle of the honey-pot and the swarm of summer flies; *you* are the pot of honey—the dollars are the flies.

"Now the honey doesn't worry about the flies, it is content to be sweet, to give off a faint sweet smell and to stick, but the flies *do* want it, they come from all quarters, they swarm into it, sip its sweetness, and buzz-zz-zz all all around. The honey is a *power*—irresistible *power* so far as flies go—they want it, it is a great center of attraction.

"Now say you run some particular line of business—you are the honey—in the world there are many people who want what you have to give them, who will gladly pay cash for it, who cannot help being attracted to your honey, as the flies might be.

"Your *thought*, as I have so often told you, is strong and potent beyond measure, but, when you assume the 'wanting' attitude, although you do most certainly *attract*, it is nothing like the powerful attraction formed by your quiet, confident attitude of absolute conviction that the thing *wants you*. The attitude of desire is strong, but the attitude of certainty—of *possession*—which this new thought makes possible is wonderful, and a veritable tower of strength; it has made things possible to me that were quite out of the question before."

Elizabeth Towne, editor of *Nautilus*, in her issue of May, 1903, copies the above from *Wings of Truth* and says:—"I reprint this item because it is too good to be missed by the thousands of American readers who never see this bright little English magazine. I believe the idea that money wants *you* will help you to the right mental condition. Be a pot of honey and let it *come*."

'NOW" FOLK,

NEW THOUGHT CENTER OF PACIFIC COAST

1437 Market Street, San Francisco, Calif.

"NOW" Folk, of which, Henry Harrison Brown is President, have associated themselves together to teach man to know himself as a manifestation of the One Infinite Energy, and how to direct this Energy, which is his sub-conscious self, in its objective expression, and thus mold his destiny to his desire. This knowledge is above all other knowledge.

An announcement of our work will be found on the following pages.

Three Epoch-Making Books

By Henry Harrison Brown.

These big-little books are having a phenomenal sale and give universal satisfaction.

How to Control Fate through Suggestion
4th Edition; 60 pp.; paper, 25c

In Part I., this book evolves the Science and Philosophy of Life; in Part II., it shows the Place and Power of Suggestion.

The principles dealt with are: Unity. Revolution. Tendency of Thought. Fate. Man. Logic. Matter. Evolution. Force. Spirit The New Man. Finer Vibrations. All Knowledge

Possible. Race Sensitiveness. Saviors. Progress.
No Sickness. Liberty. Spiritual Gifts. Classi-
fication of Psychic Power. Love. Love's Pitch
and Octaves. Concentration. Involuntary
Concentration. One Power to Heal. Millen-
nium Here.

Some Model Suggestions are given to aid the
reader to demonstrate what the book teaches.

ELLA WHEELER WILCOX has an article in the
New York Evening Journal, which also appeared in
the Chicago American and San Francisco Examiner,
in which she says: "The world is full of New Thought
Literature. It is helpful and inspiring to read. The
latest to come to me is: 'How to Control Fate
through Suggestion.,' by Henry Harrison Brown.
It is worth many dollars to any one who will LIVE
its philosophy."

EUGENE DEL MAR, Editor of Common Sense and
author of "Spiritual and Material Attraction,"
writes: "The truths are very clearly expressed and
well presented. The book is in every way quite
readable."

Not Hypnotism but Suggestion,

3d Edition; 60 pp.; paper, 25c

In this book the Law of Suggestion is evolved
and the phenomena of Hypnotism explained.
This phenomena is due to the action of the Sub-
jective mind, and should be studied until the
Art of Self-Suggestion is so perfect that the in-
dividual can make himself that which he desires.

The principles dealt with are: Truth and Unity.
Power of Choice. Sensation. Emotion. Re-
sponsibility of Choice. Where lies choice? Re-
sult of Thinking. Fate Can be Controlled.
Power of Thought. Self-Assertion. The Power
of Will. Hypnotism. Self-Suggestion. Post-
Hypnotism. Thought Seeds. Spiritualism.

Christian Science. Materialized Will. Mastery of Fate. The Manifest Ideal.

Also, several pages are devoted to formulas for self-treatment which are very valuable.

GRANT WALLACE, who is writing most valuable editorials for the evening Bulletin of this city, has twice referred to it as "a very fine little book" and recommends it to his readers as a text-book on Suggestion.

J. STITT WILSON, editor, author, and teacher of the New Thought, well known upon his own platform and that of the advanced Socialists, writes: "Your books are unique and to the point. They have the breath of life in them. I will bring them to the notice of my classes."

Man's Greatest Discovery,

3d Edition; 60 pp.; paper, 25c

Six Essays upon these subjects: Thought as Power (An Explanation and a Prophecy). Telepathy:—the Missing Link. The Ultimate of Power:—the Universe is One. Life:—Its Potential and Conservation. Vibration. The Victory Over Death:—Levitation, Materialization, De-Materialization.

The author fortifies his position with copious extracts from scientists and thinkers to show that his ideas are only supplementing the deductions of present science and in harmony with the evolutionary philosophy. It is a book to stimulate thought. It will please you.

DR. ALEX. J. McIVOR-TYNDALL, who is without a doubt the greatest demonstrator of thought-reading, says: "I would like to commend it to every person who can read. It is simple; concise; convincing No one, perhaps, knows better than I that what you state in its pages is, as you say, 'man's greatest discovery.' There is no doubt that Thought is Force capable of accomplishing what we will."

"NOW" FOLK

SOUL CULTURE INSTITUTE

Henry Harrison Brown, Instructor.

Instruction given in SUGGESTION, ART OF LIVING, and PSYCHOMETRY, which include every phase of Psychic Development. Full particulars given upon application.

For the benefit of those who cannot attend the classes at the Institute, we offer

Complete Mail Courses

on these lines of thought. In offering these courses to the public, we feel confidentin stating that nothing approaching them in value has ever been produced in the correspondence line. They are at once unique and valuable. If you are searching for a clear exposition of what is known as the New Thought, you will find this to be the fountain where you may drink and be satisfied as Mr. Brown writes from 30 years experience. A brief outline of the ground covered in each course is given below:

25 Lessons in SUGGESTION.

This course unfolds the ever-present Law of Suggestion and teaches the art of applying it. A solid foundation or starting point is given   It takes up every phase of psychic development and gives the knowl-edge that unlocks the powers of the Soul. Remem-ber that a suggestion is anything which causes an idea in the mind. It deals with basic principles; man as an ego, man and his relation to the universe and his fellows; vibration, the nervous system, philoso-phy of suggestion; the law; subject and operator, their relations; how to give, maintain, and remove a suggestion; condition of hypnosis, its relation to sleep; concentration; relations of age, occupation, temperament, disease, etc., to suggestivity; stages of hypnosis; physiology of suggestion; how to use suggestion in inhibition of pain, in cure of bad hab-its, in training of children, in business, in education, reform, and in one's own development.

25 Lessons in ART OF LIVING.

This valuable course gives the key to healing and self-development in all spiritual gifts. It is a purely scientific application of the principles underlying the systems of "Mental," "Divine," and "Christian" Science and all other schools of metaphysics. It practically covers the fundamental principles of science, the law of physics, and the dual manifesta-tions of the one substance known as matter and mind. It deals with vibration, sensation, personal magnetism, thought as a form of energy, telepathy, clairvoyance, and mental healing; how to be and keep well, the healing power of thought, self-protec-tion as sensitives, how to cultivate self-protection, inspiration, etc.

TERMS:—Each of these complete courses consists of 25 lessons, each lesson printed and bound separately and sent one at a time. Price: 50c per lesson, or $10 for a complete course if paid in advance. Mr. Brown will answer one letter of inquiry on each lesson without extra charge. This personal relation be-tween teacher and pupil adds much to these valuable courses.

N. B. –These courses have received the highest commendation from all who have studied them. The course in Suggestion should be taken up first, the Art of Living next, then we have a course in Psychometry which is yet more ad-vanced. Correspondence solicited.

Readings by Psychometry.

Psychometry is Soul-Reading. It covers all the psychic phenomena usually included under the terms Clairvoyance, Inspiration, Healing, Prophecy, Etc. It is the art of reading from the radiations each person or thing sends out from itself. We are thus put into conscious relations with the Soul, or, as it is now popular to call it, with the sub-conscious life.

Advice in business, or matters of life, and in development of any psychic phase will be given by Henry Harrison Brown. He has had 25 years' experience in this work, has never failed to read correctly, and is the most practical of advisers. He points out the possibilities of the individual from the soul-side and reveals the errors in the thought-life. These Readings are priceless to the recipient. Hundreds have testified to this fact.

Write a short letter as to a friend, giving outlines only of the desire, and enclose $1.00, and a reply will be sent at once.

TREATMENT.

HENRY HARRISON BROWN and his assistants successfully treat, through Suggestion and Higher Spiritual Power, all chronic, mental, and nervous diseases.

HABITS.

Suggestion is the best possible agent in the correction of all Habits, Vices, or weakness. All patients are educated in right thinking, thus establishing the self-confidence and reliance necessary for perfect health and mental balance.

☞ Out of town patients treated by Silent Power and instructed by letter.

Correspondence solicited. Address all communications to

"NOW" FOLK,

1437 Market St., San Francisco, Calif.